MORNING RITUAL

DAILY CHECKLIST + JOURNAL

CREATED BY EMILY ANNE BRANT

Thank you for purchasing The Ritual Journal!

Before you begin writing in your shiny new journal, there is some clarity work we need to do first. I'll walk you through some prompts so you can establish where you are and where you want to go.

We will establish your "why" – the reason behind your biggest goals and dreams- which will be your anchor when the going gets tough. You'll need to revisit your "why" each time you feel like giving up on your biggest, craziest goals, sabotaging your diet, or quitting that new workout plan. Your "why" should also be what motivates you to get out of bed each morning, just a few minutes earlier, to take this crucially important time for yourself. Do your best to never miss a day. You can complete your morning entry in as little as 5-10 minutes, so there is no excuse not to pick it up every day and expand your clarity, intention and focus. You will feel so great knowing that you are living intentionally and in alignment with the person you want to be! I am so excited for you!

Remember why and where you started and where you are going. Let's get some clarity and begin! I hope you'll love this journal as much as I do, which was created out of a desire to make a morning and evening ritual less daunting, easy to follow and easy to stick to! It was created to include all of the best, most effective prompts and notes I have collected from the past few years of my own personal growth studies.

Enjoy and get ready to grow! Xo

Emily

REALITY CHECK AND CLARITY

I WOULD CURRENTLY RATE MY PHYSICAL HEALTH AS (CIRCLE 1)

POOR   FAIR   AVERAGE   GOOD   EXCELLENT

I WOULD CURRENTLY RATE MY RELATIONSHIPS WITH OTHERS AS (CIRCLE 1)

POOR   FAIR   AVERAGE   GOOD   EXCELLENT

I WOULD CURRENTLY RATE MY CAREER OR WORK AS (CIRCLE 1)

POOR   FAIR   AVERAGE   GOOD   EXCELLENT

IF NOTHING CHANGED 5 YEARS FROM NOW, WOULD I BE HAPPY?
(Answer yes or no, and why)

BRAIN DUMP

Use the space below to write down, without judgement, all of your biggest, craziest goals and dreams or ideas! Who do you want to be, what do you want to have and what do you want to do?

GOALS AND "WHY"

Of all the goals you just wrote down, which 5 would bring you the most joy?

1

2

3

4

5

You will write these down every day where it says "5 Biggest Achievements of My Life" as if they've already happened. It is okay if they change. These are the 5 goals you will think about and write down daily, starting with just 1 to start working on first. Now, write down below why these goals are so important to YOU. This is your "why" and if it doesn't bring you to tears, keep writing until it does. It has to be about you (not your children, or all the people you're going to help) in order for you to care enough to actually achieve everything on your goal list.

MY WHY...

5 THINGS I'M GRATEFUL FOR THIS MORNING

_____

_____

_____

_____

5 BIGGEST ACHIEVEMENTS OF MY LIFE

_____

_____

_____

_____

5 TARGETS FOR TODAY

THE GOAL I'M WORKING ON FIRST:

_____

TODAY'S PROMISE TO MYSELF:

_____

TODAY'S MOVEMENT OR WORKOUT GOAL:

_____

TODAY'S AFFIRMATION:

_____

ONE ACTION I'LL TAKE TODAY TO MOVE TOWARDS MY FIRST GOAL:

_____

MORNING CHECKLIST

- ☐ DO NOT TOUCH CELL PHONE FOR MINIMUM 20 MINS
- ☐ TEA OR COFFEE
- ☐ 5 MINS POSITIVE CONTENT (PODCAST, UPLIFTING MUSIC, BOOK)
- ☐ 16oz GLASS OF WATER
- ☐ STRETCH MY BODY
- ☐ GREEN SMOOTHIE
- ☐ PRAY OR MEDITATE 2-5 MINS
- ☐ MORNING SUPPLEMENTS OR ESSENTIAL OILS
- ☐ DRESSED AND STYLED FOR SUCCESS, FULL BODY SKIN CARE DONE

I CAN VISUALIZE MY BODY AND HEALTH…

I CAN VISUALIZE MY RELATIONSHIPS…

3 WORDS I WANT PEOPLE TO DESCRIBE ME AS…

NOTES AND IDEAS

_____

_____

_____

_____

5 THINGS I'M GRATEFUL FOR THIS MORNING

---

5 BIGGEST ACHIEVEMENTS OF MY LIFE

---

5 TARGETS FOR TODAY

THE GOAL I'M WORKING ON FIRST:

TODAY'S PROMISE TO MYSELF:

TODAY'S MOVEMENT OR WORKOUT GOAL:

TODAY'S AFFIRMATION:

ONE ACTION I'LL TAKE TODAY TO MOVE TOWARDS MY FIRST GOAL:

MORNING CHECKLIST

- [ ] DO NOT TOUCH CELL PHONE FOR MINIMUM 20 MINS
- [ ] TEA OR COFFEE
- [ ] 5 MINS POSITIVE CONTENT (PODCAST, UPLIFTING MUSIC, BOOK)
- [ ] 16oz GLASS OF WATER
- [ ] STRETCH MY BODY
- [ ] GREEN SMOOTHIE
- [ ] PRAY OR MEDITATE 2-5 MINS
- [ ] MORNING SUPPLEMENTS OR ESSENTIAL OILS
- [ ] DRESSED AND STYLED FOR SUCCESS, FULL BODY SKIN CARE DONE

I CAN VISUALIZE MY BODY AND HEALTH…

I CAN VISUALIZE MY RELATIONSHIPS…

3 WORDS I WANT PEOPLE TO DESCRIBE ME AS…

NOTES AND IDEAS

_____

_____

_____

_____

5 THINGS I'M GRATEFUL FOR THIS MORNING

_____

_____

_____

_____

_____

5 BIGGEST ACHIEVEMENTS OF MY LIFE

_____

_____

_____

_____

_____

5 TARGETS FOR TODAY

THE GOAL I'M WORKING ON FIRST:

_____

TODAY'S PROMISE TO MYSELF:

_____

TODAY'S MOVEMENT OR WORKOUT GOAL:

_____

TODAY'S AFFIRMATION:

_____

ONE ACTION I'LL TAKE TODAY TO MOVE TOWARDS MY FIRST GOAL:

_____

MORNING CHECKLIST

- ☐ DO NOT TOUCH CELL PHONE FOR MINIMUM 20 MINS
- ☐ TEA OR COFFEE
- ☐ 5 MINS POSITIVE CONTENT (PODCAST, UPLIFTING MUSIC, BOOK)
- ☐ 16oz GLASS OF WATER
- ☐ STRETCH MY BODY
- ☐ GREEN SMOOTHIE
- ☐ PRAY OR MEDITATE 2-5 MINS
- ☐ MORNING SUPPLEMENTS OR ESSENTIAL OILS
- ☐ DRESSED AND STYLED FOR SUCCESS, FULL BODY SKIN CARE DONE

I CAN VISUALIZE MY BODY AND HEALTH…

I CAN VISUALIZE MY RELATIONSHIPS…

3 WORDS I WANT PEOPLE TO DESCRIBE ME AS…

NOTES AND IDEAS

_____

_____

_____

_____

5 THINGS I'M GRATEFUL FOR THIS MORNING

_____

_____

_____

_____

_____

5 BIGGEST ACHIEVEMENTS OF MY LIFE

_____

_____

_____

_____

_____

5 TARGETS FOR TODAY

THE GOAL I'M WORKING ON FIRST:

_____

TODAY'S PROMISE TO MYSELF:

_____

TODAY'S MOVEMENT OR WORKOUT GOAL:

_____

TODAY'S AFFIRMATION:

_____

ONE ACTION I'LL TAKE TODAY TO MOVE TOWARDS MY FIRST GOAL:

_____

MORNING CHECKLIST

- ☐ DO NOT TOUCH CELL PHONE FOR MINIMUM 20 MINS
- ☐ TEA OR COFFEE
- ☐ 5 MINS POSITIVE CONTENT (PODCAST, UPLIFTING MUSIC, BOOK)
- ☐ 16oz GLASS OF WATER
- ☐ STRETCH MY BODY
- ☐ GREEN SMOOTHIE
- ☐ PRAY OR MEDITATE 2-5 MINS
- ☐ MORNING SUPPLEMENTS OR ESSENTIAL OILS
- ☐ DRESSED AND STYLED FOR SUCCESS, FULL BODY SKIN CARE DONE

I CAN VISUALIZE MY BODY AND HEALTH…

I CAN VISUALIZE MY RELATIONSHIPS…

3 WORDS I WANT PEOPLE TO DESCRIBE ME AS…

NOTES AND IDEAS

_____

_____

_____

_____

5 | THINGS I'M GRATEFUL FOR THIS MORNING

_____

_____

_____

_____

_____

5 | BIGGEST ACHIEVEMENTS OF MY LIFE

_____

_____

_____

_____

_____

5 | TARGETS FOR TODAY

THE GOAL I'M WORKING ON FIRST:

_____

TODAY'S PROMISE TO MYSELF:

_____

TODAY'S MOVEMENT OR WORKOUT GOAL:

_____

TODAY'S AFFIRMATION:

_____

ONE ACTION I'LL TAKE TODAY TO MOVE TOWARDS MY FIRST GOAL:

_____

MORNING CHECKLIST

- ☐ DO NOT TOUCH CELL PHONE FOR MINIMUM 20 MINS
- ☐ TEA OR COFFEE
- ☐ 5 MINS POSITIVE CONTENT (PODCAST, UPLIFTING MUSIC, BOOK)
- ☐ 16oz GLASS OF WATER
- ☐ STRETCH MY BODY
- ☐ GREEN SMOOTHIE
- ☐ PRAY OR MEDITATE 2-5 MINS
- ☐ MORNING SUPPLEMENTS OR ESSENTIAL OILS
- ☐ DRESSED AND STYLED FOR SUCCESS, FULL BODY SKIN CARE DONE

I CAN VISUALIZE MY BODY AND HEALTH...

I CAN VISUALIZE MY RELATIONSHIPS...

3 WORDS I WANT PEOPLE TO DESCRIBE ME AS...

NOTES AND IDEAS

_____

_____

_____

_____

5 THINGS I'M GRATEFUL FOR THIS MORNING

_____

_____

_____

_____

_____

5 BIGGEST ACHIEVEMENTS OF MY LIFE

_____

_____

_____

_____

_____

5 TARGETS FOR TODAY

THE GOAL I'M WORKING ON FIRST:

_____

TODAY'S PROMISE TO MYSELF:

_____

TODAY'S MOVEMENT OR WORKOUT GOAL:

_____

TODAY'S AFFIRMATION:

_____

ONE ACTION I'LL TAKE TODAY TO MOVE TOWARDS MY FIRST GOAL:

_____

MORNING CHECKLIST

- [ ] DO NOT TOUCH CELL PHONE FOR MINIMUM 20 MINS
- [ ] TEA OR COFFEE
- [ ] 5 MINS POSITIVE CONTENT (PODCAST, UPLIFTING MUSIC, BOOK)
- [ ] 16oz GLASS OF WATER
- [ ] STRETCH MY BODY
- [ ] GREEN SMOOTHIE
- [ ] PRAY OR MEDITATE 2-5 MINS
- [ ] MORNING SUPPLEMENTS OR ESSENTIAL OILS
- [ ] DRESSED AND STYLED FOR SUCCESS, FULL BODY SKIN CARE DONE

I CAN VISUALIZE MY BODY AND HEALTH…

I CAN VISUALIZE MY RELATIONSHIPS…

3 WORDS I WANT PEOPLE TO DESCRIBE ME AS…

NOTES AND IDEAS

_____

_____

_____

_____

5 THINGS I'M GRATEFUL FOR THIS MORNING

_____

_____

_____

_____

_____

5 BIGGEST ACHIEVEMENTS OF MY LIFE

_____

_____

_____

_____

_____

5 TARGETS FOR TODAY

THE GOAL I'M WORKING ON FIRST:

_____

TODAY'S PROMISE TO MYSELF:

_____

TODAY'S MOVEMENT OR WORKOUT GOAL:

_____

TODAY'S AFFIRMATION:

_____

ONE ACTION I'LL TAKE TODAY TO MOVE TOWARDS MY FIRST GOAL:

_____

MORNING CHECKLIST

- ☐ DO NOT TOUCH CELL PHONE FOR MINIMUM 20 MINS
- ☐ TEA OR COFFEE
- ☐ 5 MINS POSITIVE CONTENT (PODCAST, UPLIFTING MUSIC, BOOK)
- ☐ 16oz GLASS OF WATER
- ☐ STRETCH MY BODY
- ☐ GREEN SMOOTHIE
- ☐ PRAY OR MEDITATE 2-5 MINS
- ☐ MORNING SUPPLEMENTS OR ESSENTIAL OILS
- ☐ DRESSED AND STYLED FOR SUCCESS, FULL BODY SKIN CARE DONE

I CAN VISUALIZE MY BODY AND HEALTH…

I CAN VISUALIZE MY RELATIONSHIPS…

3 WORDS I WANT PEOPLE TO DESCRIBE ME AS…

NOTES AND IDEAS

_____

_____

_____

_____

5 | THINGS I'M GRATEFUL FOR THIS MORNING

_____

_____

_____

_____

_____

5 | BIGGEST ACHIEVEMENTS OF MY LIFE

_____

_____

_____

_____

_____

5 | TARGETS FOR TODAY

THE GOAL I'M WORKING ON FIRST:

_____

TODAY'S PROMISE TO MYSELF:

_____

TODAY'S MOVEMENT OR WORKOUT GOAL:

_____

TODAY'S AFFIRMATION:

_____

ONE ACTION I'LL TAKE TODAY TO MOVE TOWARDS MY FIRST GOAL:

_____

MORNING CHECKLIST

- [ ] DO NOT TOUCH CELL PHONE FOR MINIMUM 20 MINS
- [ ] TEA OR COFFEE
- [ ] 5 MINS POSITIVE CONTENT (PODCAST, UPLIFTING MUSIC, BOOK)
- [ ] 16oz GLASS OF WATER
- [ ] STRETCH MY BODY
- [ ] GREEN SMOOTHIE
- [ ] PRAY OR MEDITATE 2-5 MINS
- [ ] MORNING SUPPLEMENTS OR ESSENTIAL OILS
- [ ] DRESSED AND STYLED FOR SUCCESS, FULL BODY SKIN CARE DONE

I CAN VISUALIZE MY BODY AND HEALTH…

I CAN VISUALIZE MY RELATIONSHIPS…

3 WORDS I WANT PEOPLE TO DESCRIBE ME AS…

NOTES AND IDEAS

_____

_____

_____

_____

5 THINGS I'M GRATEFUL FOR THIS MORNING

_____

_____

_____

_____

_____

5 BIGGEST ACHIEVEMENTS OF MY LIFE

_____

_____

_____

_____

_____

5 TARGETS FOR TODAY

THE GOAL I'M WORKING ON FIRST:

_____

TODAY'S PROMISE TO MYSELF:

_____

TODAY'S MOVEMENT OR WORKOUT GOAL:

_____

TODAY'S AFFIRMATION:

_____

ONE ACTION I'LL TAKE TODAY TO MOVE TOWARDS MY FIRST GOAL:

_____

MORNING CHECKLIST

- ☐ DO NOT TOUCH CELL PHONE FOR MINIMUM 20 MINS
- ☐ TEA OR COFFEE
- ☐ 5 MINS POSITIVE CONTENT (PODCAST, UPLIFTING MUSIC, BOOK)
- ☐ 16oz GLASS OF WATER
- ☐ STRETCH MY BODY
- ☐ GREEN SMOOTHIE
- ☐ PRAY OR MEDITATE 2-5 MINS
- ☐ MORNING SUPPLEMENTS OR ESSENTIAL OILS
- ☐ DRESSED AND STYLED FOR SUCCESS, FULL BODY SKIN CARE DONE

I CAN VISUALIZE MY BODY AND HEALTH…

I CAN VISUALIZE MY RELATIONSHIPS…

3 WORDS I WANT PEOPLE TO DESCRIBE ME AS…

NOTES AND IDEAS

_____

_____

_____

_____

5 THINGS I'M GRATEFUL FOR THIS MORNING

_____

_____

_____

_____

_____

5 BIGGEST ACHIEVEMENTS OF MY LIFE

_____

_____

_____

_____

_____

5 TARGETS FOR TODAY

THE GOAL I'M WORKING ON FIRST:

_____

TODAY'S PROMISE TO MYSELF:

_____

TODAY'S MOVEMENT OR WORKOUT GOAL:

_____

TODAY'S AFFIRMATION:

_____

ONE ACTION I'LL TAKE TODAY TO MOVE TOWARDS MY FIRST GOAL:

_____

MORNING CHECKLIST

- ☐ DO NOT TOUCH CELL PHONE FOR MINIMUM 20 MINS
- ☐ TEA OR COFFEE
- ☐ 5 MINS POSITIVE CONTENT (PODCAST, UPLIFTING MUSIC, BOOK)
- ☐ 16oz GLASS OF WATER
- ☐ STRETCH MY BODY
- ☐ GREEN SMOOTHIE
- ☐ PRAY OR MEDITATE 2-5 MINS
- ☐ MORNING SUPPLEMENTS OR ESSENTIAL OILS
- ☐ DRESSED AND STYLED FOR SUCCESS, FULL BODY SKIN CARE DONE

I CAN VISUALIZE MY BODY AND HEALTH...

I CAN VISUALIZE MY RELATIONSHIPS...

3 WORDS I WANT PEOPLE TO DESCRIBE ME AS...

NOTES AND IDEAS

_____

_____

_____

_____

5 THINGS I'M GRATEFUL FOR THIS MORNING

_____

_____

_____

_____

_____

5 BIGGEST ACHIEVEMENTS OF MY LIFE

_____

_____

_____

_____

_____

5 TARGETS FOR TODAY

THE GOAL I'M WORKING ON FIRST:

_____

TODAY'S PROMISE TO MYSELF:

_____

TODAY'S MOVEMENT OR WORKOUT GOAL:

_____

TODAY'S AFFIRMATION:

_____

ONE ACTION I'LL TAKE TODAY TO MOVE TOWARDS MY FIRST GOAL:

_____

MORNING CHECKLIST

- ☐ DO NOT TOUCH CELL PHONE FOR MINIMUM 20 MINS
- ☐ TEA OR COFFEE
- ☐ 5 MINS POSITIVE CONTENT (PODCAST, UPLIFTING MUSIC, BOOK)
- ☐ 16oz GLASS OF WATER
- ☐ STRETCH MY BODY
- ☐ GREEN SMOOTHIE
- ☐ PRAY OR MEDITATE 2-5 MINS
- ☐ MORNING SUPPLEMENTS OR ESSENTIAL OILS
- ☐ DRESSED AND STYLED FOR SUCCESS, FULL BODY SKIN CARE DONE

I CAN VISUALIZE MY BODY AND HEALTH...

I CAN VISUALIZE MY RELATIONSHIPS...

3 WORDS I WANT PEOPLE TO DESCRIBE ME AS...

NOTES AND IDEAS

_____

_____

_____

_____

5 THINGS I'M GRATEFUL FOR THIS MORNING

_____

_____

_____

_____

_____

5 BIGGEST ACHIEVEMENTS OF MY LIFE

_____

_____

_____

_____

_____

5 TARGETS FOR TODAY

THE GOAL I'M WORKING ON FIRST:

_____

TODAY'S PROMISE TO MYSELF:

_____

TODAY'S MOVEMENT OR WORKOUT GOAL:

_____

TODAY'S AFFIRMATION:

_____

ONE ACTION I'LL TAKE TODAY TO MOVE TOWARDS MY FIRST GOAL:

_____

MORNING CHECKLIST

- ☐ DO NOT TOUCH CELL PHONE FOR MINIMUM 20 MINS
- ☐ TEA OR COFFEE
- ☐ 5 MINS POSITIVE CONTENT (PODCAST, UPLIFTING MUSIC, BOOK)
- ☐ 16oz GLASS OF WATER
- ☐ STRETCH MY BODY
- ☐ GREEN SMOOTHIE
- ☐ PRAY OR MEDITATE 2-5 MINS
- ☐ MORNING SUPPLEMENTS OR ESSENTIAL OILS
- ☐ DRESSED AND STYLED FOR SUCCESS, FULL BODY SKIN CARE DONE

I CAN VISUALIZE MY BODY AND HEALTH...

I CAN VISUALIZE MY RELATIONSHIPS...

3 WORDS I WANT PEOPLE TO DESCRIBE ME AS...

NOTES AND IDEAS

_____

_____

_____

_____

5 THINGS I'M GRATEFUL FOR THIS MORNING

_____

_____

_____

_____

_____

5 BIGGEST ACHIEVEMENTS OF MY LIFE

_____

_____

_____

_____

_____

5 TARGETS FOR TODAY

THE GOAL I'M WORKING ON FIRST:

_____

TODAY'S PROMISE TO MYSELF:

_____

TODAY'S MOVEMENT OR WORKOUT GOAL:

_____

TODAY'S AFFIRMATION:

_____

ONE ACTION I'LL TAKE TODAY TO MOVE TOWARDS MY FIRST GOAL:

_____

MORNING CHECKLIST

- [ ] DO NOT TOUCH CELL PHONE FOR MINIMUM 20 MINS
- [ ] TEA OR COFFEE
- [ ] 5 MINS POSITIVE CONTENT (PODCAST, UPLIFTING MUSIC, BOOK)
- [ ] 16oz GLASS OF WATER
- [ ] STRETCH MY BODY
- [ ] GREEN SMOOTHIE
- [ ] PRAY OR MEDITATE 2-5 MINS
- [ ] MORNING SUPPLEMENTS OR ESSENTIAL OILS
- [ ] DRESSED AND STYLED FOR SUCCESS, FULL BODY SKIN CARE DONE

I CAN VISUALIZE MY BODY AND HEALTH...

I CAN VISUALIZE MY RELATIONSHIPS...

3 WORDS I WANT PEOPLE TO DESCRIBE ME AS...

NOTES AND IDEAS

_____

_____

_____

_____

5 THINGS I'M GRATEFUL FOR THIS MORNING

_____

_____

_____

_____

_____

5 BIGGEST ACHIEVEMENTS OF MY LIFE

_____

_____

_____

_____

_____

5 TARGETS FOR TODAY

THE GOAL I'M WORKING ON FIRST:

_____

TODAY'S PROMISE TO MYSELF:

_____

TODAY'S MOVEMENT OR WORKOUT GOAL:

_____

TODAY'S AFFIRMATION:

_____

ONE ACTION I'LL TAKE TODAY TO MOVE TOWARDS MY FIRST GOAL:

_____

MORNING CHECKLIST

- ☐ DO NOT TOUCH CELL PHONE FOR MINIMUM 20 MINS
- ☐ TEA OR COFFEE
- ☐ 5 MINS POSITIVE CONTENT (PODCAST, UPLIFTING MUSIC, BOOK)
- ☐ 16oz GLASS OF WATER
- ☐ STRETCH MY BODY
- ☐ GREEN SMOOTHIE
- ☐ PRAY OR MEDITATE 2-5 MINS
- ☐ MORNING SUPPLEMENTS OR ESSENTIAL OILS
- ☐ DRESSED AND STYLED FOR SUCCESS, FULL BODY SKIN CARE DONE

I CAN VISUALIZE MY BODY AND HEALTH...

I CAN VISUALIZE MY RELATIONSHIPS...

3 WORDS I WANT PEOPLE TO DESCRIBE ME AS...

NOTES AND IDEAS

_____

_____

_____

_____

5 THINGS I'M GRATEFUL FOR THIS MORNING

---

5 BIGGEST ACHIEVEMENTS OF MY LIFE

---

5 TARGETS FOR TODAY

THE GOAL I'M WORKING ON FIRST:

TODAY'S PROMISE TO MYSELF:

TODAY'S MOVEMENT OR WORKOUT GOAL:

TODAY'S AFFIRMATION:

ONE ACTION I'LL TAKE TODAY TO MOVE TOWARDS MY FIRST GOAL:

MORNING CHECKLIST

- ☐ DO NOT TOUCH CELL PHONE FOR MINIMUM 20 MINS
- ☐ TEA OR COFFEE
- ☐ 5 MINS POSITIVE CONTENT (PODCAST, UPLIFTING MUSIC, BOOK)
- ☐ 16oz GLASS OF WATER
- ☐ STRETCH MY BODY
- ☐ GREEN SMOOTHIE
- ☐ PRAY OR MEDITATE 2-5 MINS
- ☐ MORNING SUPPLEMENTS OR ESSENTIAL OILS
- ☐ DRESSED AND STYLED FOR SUCCESS, FULL BODY SKIN CARE DONE

I CAN VISUALIZE MY BODY AND HEALTH…

I CAN VISUALIZE MY RELATIONSHIPS…

3 WORDS I WANT PEOPLE TO DESCRIBE ME AS…

NOTES AND IDEAS

_____

_____

_____

_____

5 | THINGS I'M GRATEFUL FOR THIS MORNING

_____

_____

_____

_____

_____

5 | BIGGEST ACHIEVEMENTS OF MY LIFE

_____

_____

_____

_____

_____

5 | TARGETS FOR TODAY

THE GOAL I'M WORKING ON FIRST:

_____

TODAY'S PROMISE TO MYSELF:

_____

TODAY'S MOVEMENT OR WORKOUT GOAL:

_____

TODAY'S AFFIRMATION:

_____

ONE ACTION I'LL TAKE TODAY TO MOVE TOWARDS MY FIRST GOAL:

_____

MORNING CHECKLIST

- ☐ DO NOT TOUCH CELL PHONE FOR MINIMUM 20 MINS
- ☐ TEA OR COFFEE
- ☐ 5 MINS POSITIVE CONTENT (PODCAST, UPLIFTING MUSIC, BOOK)
- ☐ 16oz GLASS OF WATER
- ☐ STRETCH MY BODY
- ☐ GREEN SMOOTHIE
- ☐ PRAY OR MEDITATE 2-5 MINS
- ☐ MORNING SUPPLEMENTS OR ESSENTIAL OILS
- ☐ DRESSED AND STYLED FOR SUCCESS, FULL BODY SKIN CARE DONE

I CAN VISUALIZE MY BODY AND HEALTH...

I CAN VISUALIZE MY RELATIONSHIPS...

3 WORDS I WANT PEOPLE TO DESCRIBE ME AS...

NOTES AND IDEAS

_____

_____

_____

_____

5 THINGS I'M GRATEFUL FOR THIS MORNING

_____

_____

_____

_____

_____

5 BIGGEST ACHIEVEMENTS OF MY LIFE

_____

_____

_____

_____

_____

5 TARGETS FOR TODAY

THE GOAL I'M WORKING ON FIRST:

_____

TODAY'S PROMISE TO MYSELF:

_____

TODAY'S MOVEMENT OR WORKOUT GOAL:

_____

TODAY'S AFFIRMATION:

_____

ONE ACTION I'LL TAKE TODAY TO MOVE TOWARDS MY FIRST GOAL:

_____

MORNING CHECKLIST

- ☐ DO NOT TOUCH CELL PHONE FOR MINIMUM 20 MINS
- ☐ TEA OR COFFEE
- ☐ 5 MINS POSITIVE CONTENT (PODCAST, UPLIFTING MUSIC, BOOK)
- ☐ 16oz GLASS OF WATER
- ☐ STRETCH MY BODY
- ☐ GREEN SMOOTHIE
- ☐ PRAY OR MEDITATE 2-5 MINS
- ☐ MORNING SUPPLEMENTS OR ESSENTIAL OILS
- ☐ DRESSED AND STYLED FOR SUCCESS, FULL BODY SKIN CARE DONE

I CAN VISUALIZE MY BODY AND HEALTH...

I CAN VISUALIZE MY RELATIONSHIPS...

3 WORDS I WANT PEOPLE TO DESCRIBE ME AS...

NOTES AND IDEAS

_____

_____

_____

_____

5 THINGS I'M GRATEFUL FOR THIS MORNING

5 BIGGEST ACHIEVEMENTS OF MY LIFE

_____

_____

_____

_____

_____

_____

_____

_____

_____

_____

5 TARGETS FOR TODAY

THE GOAL I'M WORKING ON FIRST:

_____

TODAY'S PROMISE TO MYSELF:

_____

TODAY'S MOVEMENT OR WORKOUT GOAL:

_____

TODAY'S AFFIRMATION:

_____

ONE ACTION I'LL TAKE TODAY TO MOVE TOWARDS MY FIRST GOAL:

_____

MORNING CHECKLIST

- ☐ DO NOT TOUCH CELL PHONE FOR MINIMUM 20 MINS
- ☐ TEA OR COFFEE
- ☐ 5 MINS POSITIVE CONTENT (PODCAST, UPLIFTING MUSIC, BOOK)
- ☐ 16oz GLASS OF WATER
- ☐ STRETCH MY BODY
- ☐ GREEN SMOOTHIE
- ☐ PRAY OR MEDITATE 2-5 MINS
- ☐ MORNING SUPPLEMENTS OR ESSENTIAL OILS
- ☐ DRESSED AND STYLED FOR SUCCESS, FULL BODY SKIN CARE DONE

I CAN VISUALIZE MY BODY AND HEALTH…

I CAN VISUALIZE MY RELATIONSHIPS…

3 WORDS I WANT PEOPLE TO DESCRIBE ME AS…

NOTES AND IDEAS

_____

_____

_____

_____

5 THINGS I'M GRATEFUL FOR THIS MORNING

_____

_____

_____

_____

_____

5 BIGGEST ACHIEVEMENTS OF MY LIFE

_____

_____

_____

_____

_____

5 TARGETS FOR TODAY

THE GOAL I'M WORKING ON FIRST:

_____

TODAY'S PROMISE TO MYSELF:

_____

TODAY'S MOVEMENT OR WORKOUT GOAL:

_____

TODAY'S AFFIRMATION:

_____

ONE ACTION I'LL TAKE TODAY TO MOVE TOWARDS MY FIRST GOAL:

_____

MORNING CHECKLIST

- ☐ DO NOT TOUCH CELL PHONE FOR MINIMUM 20 MINS
- ☐ TEA OR COFFEE
- ☐ 5 MINS POSITIVE CONTENT (PODCAST, UPLIFTING MUSIC, BOOK)
- ☐ 16oz GLASS OF WATER
- ☐ STRETCH MY BODY
- ☐ GREEN SMOOTHIE
- ☐ PRAY OR MEDITATE 2-5 MINS
- ☐ MORNING SUPPLEMENTS OR ESSENTIAL OILS
- ☐ DRESSED AND STYLED FOR SUCCESS, FULL BODY SKIN CARE DONE

I CAN VISUALIZE MY BODY AND HEALTH…

I CAN VISUALIZE MY RELATIONSHIPS…

3 WORDS I WANT PEOPLE TO DESCRIBE ME AS…

NOTES AND IDEAS

_____

_____

_____

_____

5 THINGS I'M GRATEFUL FOR THIS MORNING

_____

_____

_____

_____

_____

5 BIGGEST ACHIEVEMENTS OF MY LIFE

_____

_____

_____

_____

_____

5 TARGETS FOR TODAY

THE GOAL I'M WORKING ON FIRST:

_____

TODAY'S PROMISE TO MYSELF:

_____

TODAY'S MOVEMENT OR WORKOUT GOAL:

_____

TODAY'S AFFIRMATION:

_____

ONE ACTION I'LL TAKE TODAY TO MOVE TOWARDS MY FIRST GOAL:

_____

MORNING CHECKLIST

- ☐ DO NOT TOUCH CELL PHONE FOR MINIMUM 20 MINS
- ☐ TEA OR COFFEE
- ☐ 5 MINS POSITIVE CONTENT (PODCAST, UPLIFTING MUSIC, BOOK)
- ☐ 16oz GLASS OF WATER
- ☐ STRETCH MY BODY
- ☐ GREEN SMOOTHIE
- ☐ PRAY OR MEDITATE 2-5 MINS
- ☐ MORNING SUPPLEMENTS OR ESSENTIAL OILS
- ☐ DRESSED AND STYLED FOR SUCCESS, FULL BODY SKIN CARE DONE

I CAN VISUALIZE MY BODY AND HEALTH...

I CAN VISUALIZE MY RELATIONSHIPS...

3 WORDS I WANT PEOPLE TO DESCRIBE ME AS...

NOTES AND IDEAS

_____

_____

_____

_____

5 THINGS I'M GRATEFUL FOR THIS MORNING

_____

_____

_____

_____

_____

5 BIGGEST ACHIEVEMENTS OF MY LIFE

_____

_____

_____

_____

_____

5 TARGETS FOR TODAY

THE GOAL I'M WORKING ON FIRST:

_____

TODAY'S PROMISE TO MYSELF:

_____

TODAY'S MOVEMENT OR WORKOUT GOAL:

_____

TODAY'S AFFIRMATION:

_____

ONE ACTION I'LL TAKE TODAY TO MOVE TOWARDS MY FIRST GOAL:

_____

MORNING CHECKLIST

- ☐ DO NOT TOUCH CELL PHONE FOR MINIMUM 20 MINS
- ☐ TEA OR COFFEE
- ☐ 5 MINS POSITIVE CONTENT (PODCAST, UPLIFTING MUSIC, BOOK)
- ☐ 16oz GLASS OF WATER
- ☐ STRETCH MY BODY
- ☐ GREEN SMOOTHIE
- ☐ PRAY OR MEDITATE 2-5 MINS
- ☐ MORNING SUPPLEMENTS OR ESSENTIAL OILS
- ☐ DRESSED AND STYLED FOR SUCCESS, FULL BODY SKIN CARE DONE

I CAN VISUALIZE MY BODY AND HEALTH...

I CAN VISUALIZE MY RELATIONSHIPS...

3 WORDS I WANT PEOPLE TO DESCRIBE ME AS...

NOTES AND IDEAS

_____

_____

_____

_____

5 | THINGS I'M GRATEFUL FOR THIS MORNING

_____

_____

_____

_____

_____

5 | BIGGEST ACHIEVEMENTS OF MY LIFE

_____

_____

_____

_____

_____

5 | TARGETS FOR TODAY

THE GOAL I'M WORKING ON FIRST:

_____

TODAY'S PROMISE TO MYSELF:

_____

TODAY'S MOVEMENT OR WORKOUT GOAL:

_____

TODAY'S AFFIRMATION:

_____

ONE ACTION I'LL TAKE TODAY TO MOVE TOWARDS MY FIRST GOAL:

_____

MORNING CHECKLIST

- ☐ DO NOT TOUCH CELL PHONE FOR MINIMUM 20 MINS
- ☐ TEA OR COFFEE
- ☐ 5 MINS POSITIVE CONTENT (PODCAST, UPLIFTING MUSIC, BOOK)
- ☐ 16oz GLASS OF WATER
- ☐ STRETCH MY BODY
- ☐ GREEN SMOOTHIE
- ☐ PRAY OR MEDITATE 2-5 MINS
- ☐ MORNING SUPPLEMENTS OR ESSENTIAL OILS
- ☐ DRESSED AND STYLED FOR SUCCESS, FULL BODY SKIN CARE DONE

I CAN VISUALIZE MY BODY AND HEALTH…

I CAN VISUALIZE MY RELATIONSHIPS…

3 WORDS I WANT PEOPLE TO DESCRIBE ME AS…

NOTES AND IDEAS

_____

_____

_____

_____

5 THINGS I'M GRATEFUL FOR THIS MORNING

_____

_____

_____

_____

_____

5 BIGGEST ACHIEVEMENTS OF MY LIFE

_____

_____

_____

_____

_____

5 TARGETS FOR TODAY

THE GOAL I'M WORKING ON FIRST:

_____

TODAY'S PROMISE TO MYSELF:

_____

TODAY'S MOVEMENT OR WORKOUT GOAL:

_____

TODAY'S AFFIRMATION:

_____

ONE ACTION I'LL TAKE TODAY TO MOVE TOWARDS MY FIRST GOAL:

_____

MORNING CHECKLIST

- [ ] DO NOT TOUCH CELL PHONE FOR MINIMUM 20 MINS
- [ ] TEA OR COFFEE
- [ ] 5 MINS POSITIVE CONTENT (PODCAST, UPLIFTING MUSIC, BOOK)
- [ ] 16oz GLASS OF WATER
- [ ] STRETCH MY BODY
- [ ] GREEN SMOOTHIE
- [ ] PRAY OR MEDITATE 2-5 MINS
- [ ] MORNING SUPPLEMENTS OR ESSENTIAL OILS
- [ ] DRESSED AND STYLED FOR SUCCESS, FULL BODY SKIN CARE DONE

I CAN VISUALIZE MY BODY AND HEALTH…

I CAN VISUALIZE MY RELATIONSHIPS…

3 WORDS I WANT PEOPLE TO DESCRIBE ME AS…

NOTES AND IDEAS

_____

_____

_____

_____

5 | THINGS I'M GRATEFUL FOR THIS MORNING

_____

_____

_____

_____

_____

5 | BIGGEST ACHIEVEMENTS OF MY LIFE

_____

_____

_____

_____

_____

5 | TARGETS FOR TODAY

THE GOAL I'M WORKING ON FIRST:

_____

TODAY'S PROMISE TO MYSELF:

_____

TODAY'S MOVEMENT OR WORKOUT GOAL:

_____

TODAY'S AFFIRMATION:

_____

ONE ACTION I'LL TAKE TODAY TO MOVE TOWARDS MY FIRST GOAL:

_____

MORNING CHECKLIST

- ☐ DO NOT TOUCH CELL PHONE FOR MINIMUM 20 MINS
- ☐ TEA OR COFFEE
- ☐ 5 MINS POSITIVE CONTENT (PODCAST, UPLIFTING MUSIC, BOOK)
- ☐ 16oz GLASS OF WATER
- ☐ STRETCH MY BODY
- ☐ GREEN SMOOTHIE
- ☐ PRAY OR MEDITATE 2-5 MINS
- ☐ MORNING SUPPLEMENTS OR ESSENTIAL OILS
- ☐ DRESSED AND STYLED FOR SUCCESS, FULL BODY SKIN CARE DONE

I CAN VISUALIZE MY BODY AND HEALTH…

I CAN VISUALIZE MY RELATIONSHIPS…

3 WORDS I WANT PEOPLE TO DESCRIBE ME AS…

NOTES AND IDEAS

_____

_____

_____

_____

5 | THINGS I'M GRATEFUL FOR THIS MORNING

_____

_____

_____

_____

_____

5 | BIGGEST ACHIEVEMENTS OF MY LIFE

_____

_____

_____

_____

_____

5 | TARGETS FOR TODAY

THE GOAL I'M WORKING ON FIRST:

_____

TODAY'S PROMISE TO MYSELF:

_____

TODAY'S MOVEMENT OR WORKOUT GOAL:

_____

TODAY'S AFFIRMATION:

_____

ONE ACTION I'LL TAKE TODAY TO MOVE TOWARDS MY FIRST GOAL:

_____

MORNING CHECKLIST

- ☐ DO NOT TOUCH CELL PHONE FOR MINIMUM 20 MINS
- ☐ TEA OR COFFEE
- ☐ 5 MINS POSITIVE CONTENT (PODCAST, UPLIFTING MUSIC, BOOK)
- ☐ 16oz GLASS OF WATER
- ☐ STRETCH MY BODY
- ☐ GREEN SMOOTHIE
- ☐ PRAY OR MEDITATE 2-5 MINS
- ☐ MORNING SUPPLEMENTS OR ESSENTIAL OILS
- ☐ DRESSED AND STYLED FOR SUCCESS, FULL BODY SKIN CARE DONE

I CAN VISUALIZE MY BODY AND HEALTH...

I CAN VISUALIZE MY RELATIONSHIPS...

3 WORDS I WANT PEOPLE TO DESCRIBE ME AS...

NOTES AND IDEAS

_____

_____

_____

_____

5 THINGS I'M GRATEFUL FOR THIS MORNING

5 BIGGEST ACHIEVEMENTS OF MY LIFE

_____	_____
_____	_____
_____	_____
_____	_____
_____	_____

5 TARGETS FOR TODAY

THE GOAL I'M WORKING ON FIRST:

_____

TODAY'S PROMISE TO MYSELF:

_____

TODAY'S MOVEMENT OR WORKOUT GOAL:

_____

TODAY'S AFFIRMATION:

_____

ONE ACTION I'LL TAKE TODAY TO MOVE TOWARDS MY FIRST GOAL:

_____

MORNING CHECKLIST

- ☐ DO NOT TOUCH CELL PHONE FOR MINIMUM 20 MINS
- ☐ TEA OR COFFEE
- ☐ 5 MINS POSITIVE CONTENT (PODCAST, UPLIFTING MUSIC, BOOK)
- ☐ 16oz GLASS OF WATER
- ☐ STRETCH MY BODY
- ☐ GREEN SMOOTHIE
- ☐ PRAY OR MEDITATE 2-5 MINS
- ☐ MORNING SUPPLEMENTS OR ESSENTIAL OILS
- ☐ DRESSED AND STYLED FOR SUCCESS, FULL BODY SKIN CARE DONE

I CAN VISUALIZE MY BODY AND HEALTH...

I CAN VISUALIZE MY RELATIONSHIPS...

3 WORDS I WANT PEOPLE TO DESCRIBE ME AS...

NOTES AND IDEAS

_____

_____

_____

_____

5 | THINGS I'M GRATEFUL FOR THIS MORNING

_____

_____

_____

_____

_____

5 | BIGGEST ACHIEVEMENTS OF MY LIFE

_____

_____

_____

_____

_____

5 | TARGETS FOR TODAY

THE GOAL I'M WORKING ON FIRST:

_____

TODAY'S PROMISE TO MYSELF:

_____

TODAY'S MOVEMENT OR WORKOUT GOAL:

_____

TODAY'S AFFIRMATION:

_____

ONE ACTION I'LL TAKE TODAY TO MOVE TOWARDS MY FIRST GOAL:

_____

MORNING CHECKLIST

- ☐ DO NOT TOUCH CELL PHONE FOR MINIMUM 20 MINS
- ☐ TEA OR COFFEE
- ☐ 5 MINS POSITIVE CONTENT (PODCAST, UPLIFTING MUSIC, BOOK)
- ☐ 16oz GLASS OF WATER
- ☐ STRETCH MY BODY
- ☐ GREEN SMOOTHIE
- ☐ PRAY OR MEDITATE 2-5 MINS
- ☐ MORNING SUPPLEMENTS OR ESSENTIAL OILS
- ☐ DRESSED AND STYLED FOR SUCCESS, FULL BODY SKIN CARE DONE

I CAN VISUALIZE MY BODY AND HEALTH...

I CAN VISUALIZE MY RELATIONSHIPS...

3 WORDS I WANT PEOPLE TO DESCRIBE ME AS...

NOTES AND IDEAS

_____

_____

_____

_____

5 | THINGS I'M GRATEFUL FOR THIS MORNING

_____

_____

_____

_____

_____

5 | BIGGEST ACHIEVEMENTS OF MY LIFE

_____

_____

_____

_____

_____

5 | TARGETS FOR TODAY

THE GOAL I'M WORKING ON FIRST:

_____

TODAY'S PROMISE TO MYSELF:

_____

TODAY'S MOVEMENT OR WORKOUT GOAL:

_____

TODAY'S AFFIRMATION:

_____

ONE ACTION I'LL TAKE TODAY TO MOVE TOWARDS MY FIRST GOAL:

_____

MORNING CHECKLIST

- ☐ DO NOT TOUCH CELL PHONE FOR MINIMUM 20 MINS
- ☐ TEA OR COFFEE
- ☐ 5 MINS POSITIVE CONTENT (PODCAST, UPLIFTING MUSIC, BOOK)
- ☐ 16oz GLASS OF WATER
- ☐ STRETCH MY BODY
- ☐ GREEN SMOOTHIE
- ☐ PRAY OR MEDITATE 2-5 MINS
- ☐ MORNING SUPPLEMENTS OR ESSENTIAL OILS
- ☐ DRESSED AND STYLED FOR SUCCESS, FULL BODY SKIN CARE DONE

I CAN VISUALIZE MY BODY AND HEALTH...

I CAN VISUALIZE MY RELATIONSHIPS...

3 WORDS I WANT PEOPLE TO DESCRIBE ME AS...

NOTES AND IDEAS

_____

_____

_____

_____

5 THINGS I'M GRATEFUL FOR THIS MORNING

_____

_____

_____

_____

_____

5 BIGGEST ACHIEVEMENTS OF MY LIFE

_____

_____

_____

_____

_____

5 TARGETS FOR TODAY

THE GOAL I'M WORKING ON FIRST:

_____

TODAY'S PROMISE TO MYSELF:

_____

TODAY'S MOVEMENT OR WORKOUT GOAL:

_____

TODAY'S AFFIRMATION:

_____

ONE ACTION I'LL TAKE TODAY TO MOVE TOWARDS MY FIRST GOAL:

_____

MORNING CHECKLIST

- ☐ DO NOT TOUCH CELL PHONE FOR MINIMUM 20 MINS
- ☐ TEA OR COFFEE
- ☐ 5 MINS POSITIVE CONTENT (PODCAST, UPLIFTING MUSIC, BOOK)
- ☐ 16oz GLASS OF WATER
- ☐ STRETCH MY BODY
- ☐ GREEN SMOOTHIE
- ☐ PRAY OR MEDITATE 2-5 MINS
- ☐ MORNING SUPPLEMENTS OR ESSENTIAL OILS
- ☐ DRESSED AND STYLED FOR SUCCESS, FULL BODY SKIN CARE DONE

I CAN VISUALIZE MY BODY AND HEALTH...

I CAN VISUALIZE MY RELATIONSHIPS...

3 WORDS I WANT PEOPLE TO DESCRIBE ME AS...

NOTES AND IDEAS

_____

_____

_____

_____

5 | THINGS I'M GRATEFUL FOR THIS MORNING

_____

_____

_____

_____

_____

5 | BIGGEST ACHIEVEMENTS OF MY LIFE

_____

_____

_____

_____

_____

5 | TARGETS FOR TODAY

THE GOAL I'M WORKING ON FIRST:

_____

TODAY'S PROMISE TO MYSELF:

_____

TODAY'S MOVEMENT OR WORKOUT GOAL:

_____

TODAY'S AFFIRMATION:

_____

ONE ACTION I'LL TAKE TODAY TO MOVE TOWARDS MY FIRST GOAL:

_____

MORNING CHECKLIST

- ☐ DO NOT TOUCH CELL PHONE FOR MINIMUM 20 MINS
- ☐ TEA OR COFFEE
- ☐ 5 MINS POSITIVE CONTENT (PODCAST, UPLIFTING MUSIC, BOOK)
- ☐ 16oz GLASS OF WATER
- ☐ STRETCH MY BODY
- ☐ GREEN SMOOTHIE
- ☐ PRAY OR MEDITATE 2-5 MINS
- ☐ MORNING SUPPLEMENTS OR ESSENTIAL OILS
- ☐ DRESSED AND STYLED FOR SUCCESS, FULL BODY SKIN CARE DONE

I CAN VISUALIZE MY BODY AND HEALTH...

I CAN VISUALIZE MY RELATIONSHIPS...

3 WORDS I WANT PEOPLE TO DESCRIBE ME AS...

NOTES AND IDEAS

_____

_____

_____

_____

5 THINGS I'M GRATEFUL FOR THIS MORNING

_____

_____

_____

_____

5 BIGGEST ACHIEVEMENTS OF MY LIFE

_____

_____

_____

_____

5 TARGETS FOR TODAY

THE GOAL I'M WORKING ON FIRST:

_____

TODAY'S PROMISE TO MYSELF:

_____

TODAY'S MOVEMENT OR WORKOUT GOAL:

_____

TODAY'S AFFIRMATION:

_____

ONE ACTION I'LL TAKE TODAY TO MOVE TOWARDS MY FIRST GOAL:

_____

MORNING CHECKLIST

- ☐ DO NOT TOUCH CELL PHONE FOR MINIMUM 20 MINS
- ☐ TEA OR COFFEE
- ☐ 5 MINS POSITIVE CONTENT (PODCAST, UPLIFTING MUSIC, BOOK)
- ☐ 16oz GLASS OF WATER
- ☐ STRETCH MY BODY
- ☐ GREEN SMOOTHIE
- ☐ PRAY OR MEDITATE 2-5 MINS
- ☐ MORNING SUPPLEMENTS OR ESSENTIAL OILS
- ☐ DRESSED AND STYLED FOR SUCCESS, FULL BODY SKIN CARE DONE

I CAN VISUALIZE MY BODY AND HEALTH...

I CAN VISUALIZE MY RELATIONSHIPS...

3 WORDS I WANT PEOPLE TO DESCRIBE ME AS...

NOTES AND IDEAS

_____

_____

_____

_____

5 THINGS I'M GRATEFUL FOR THIS MORNING

_____

_____

_____

_____

_____

5 BIGGEST ACHIEVEMENTS OF MY LIFE

_____

_____

_____

_____

_____

5 TARGETS FOR TODAY

THE GOAL I'M WORKING ON FIRST:

_____

TODAY'S PROMISE TO MYSELF:

_____

TODAY'S MOVEMENT OR WORKOUT GOAL:

_____

TODAY'S AFFIRMATION:

_____

ONE ACTION I'LL TAKE TODAY TO MOVE TOWARDS MY FIRST GOAL:

_____

MORNING CHECKLIST

- ☐ DO NOT TOUCH CELL PHONE FOR MINIMUM 20 MINS
- ☐ TEA OR COFFEE
- ☐ 5 MINS POSITIVE CONTENT (PODCAST, UPLIFTING MUSIC, BOOK)
- ☐ 16oz GLASS OF WATER
- ☐ STRETCH MY BODY
- ☐ GREEN SMOOTHIE
- ☐ PRAY OR MEDITATE 2-5 MINS
- ☐ MORNING SUPPLEMENTS OR ESSENTIAL OILS
- ☐ DRESSED AND STYLED FOR SUCCESS, FULL BODY SKIN CARE DONE

I CAN VISUALIZE MY BODY AND HEALTH...

I CAN VISUALIZE MY RELATIONSHIPS...

3 WORDS I WANT PEOPLE TO DESCRIBE ME AS...

NOTES AND IDEAS

_____

_____

_____

_____

5 | THINGS I'M GRATEFUL FOR THIS MORNING

_____

_____

_____

_____

_____

5 | BIGGEST ACHIEVEMENTS OF MY LIFE

_____

_____

_____

_____

_____

5 | TARGETS FOR TODAY

THE GOAL I'M WORKING ON FIRST:

_____

TODAY'S PROMISE TO MYSELF:

_____

TODAY'S MOVEMENT OR WORKOUT GOAL:

_____

TODAY'S AFFIRMATION:

_____

ONE ACTION I'LL TAKE TODAY TO MOVE TOWARDS MY FIRST GOAL:

_____

MORNING CHECKLIST

- [ ] DO NOT TOUCH CELL PHONE FOR MINIMUM 20 MINS
- [ ] TEA OR COFFEE
- [ ] 5 MINS POSITIVE CONTENT (PODCAST, UPLIFTING MUSIC, BOOK)
- [ ] 16oz GLASS OF WATER
- [ ] STRETCH MY BODY
- [ ] GREEN SMOOTHIE
- [ ] PRAY OR MEDITATE 2-5 MINS
- [ ] MORNING SUPPLEMENTS OR ESSENTIAL OILS
- [ ] DRESSED AND STYLED FOR SUCCESS, FULL BODY SKIN CARE DONE

I CAN VISUALIZE MY BODY AND HEALTH…

I CAN VISUALIZE MY RELATIONSHIPS…

3 WORDS I WANT PEOPLE TO DESCRIBE ME AS…

NOTES AND IDEAS

_____

_____

_____

_____

5 THINGS I'M GRATEFUL FOR
THIS MORNING

5 BIGGEST ACHIEVEMENTS
OF MY LIFE

_____

_____

_____

_____

_____

_____

_____

_____

5 TARGETS FOR TODAY

THE GOAL I'M WORKING ON FIRST:

_____

TODAY'S PROMISE TO MYSELF:

_____

TODAY'S MOVEMENT OR WORKOUT GOAL:

_____

TODAY'S AFFIRMATION:

_____

ONE ACTION I'LL TAKE TODAY TO MOVE TOWARDS MY FIRST GOAL:

_____

MORNING CHECKLIST

- ☐ DO NOT TOUCH CELL PHONE FOR MINIMUM 20 MINS
- ☐ TEA OR COFFEE
- ☐ 5 MINS POSITIVE CONTENT (PODCAST, UPLIFTING MUSIC, BOOK)
- ☐ 16oz GLASS OF WATER
- ☐ STRETCH MY BODY
- ☐ GREEN SMOOTHIE
- ☐ PRAY OR MEDITATE 2-5 MINS
- ☐ MORNING SUPPLEMENTS OR ESSENTIAL OILS
- ☐ DRESSED AND STYLED FOR SUCCESS, FULL BODY SKIN CARE DONE

I CAN VISUALIZE MY BODY AND HEALTH...

I CAN VISUALIZE MY RELATIONSHIPS...

3 WORDS I WANT PEOPLE TO DESCRIBE ME AS...

NOTES AND IDEAS

_____

_____

_____

_____

5 THINGS I'M GRATEFUL FOR
THIS MORNING

5 BIGGEST ACHIEVEMENTS
OF MY LIFE

_____

_____

_____

_____

_____

_____

_____

_____

_____

_____

5 TARGETS FOR TODAY

THE GOAL I'M WORKING ON FIRST:

_____

TODAY'S PROMISE TO MYSELF:

_____

TODAY'S MOVEMENT OR WORKOUT GOAL:

_____

TODAY'S AFFIRMATION:

_____

ONE ACTION I'LL TAKE TODAY TO MOVE TOWARDS MY FIRST GOAL:

_____

MORNING CHECKLIST

- ☐ DO NOT TOUCH CELL PHONE FOR MINIMUM 20 MINS
- ☐ TEA OR COFFEE
- ☐ 5 MINS POSITIVE CONTENT (PODCAST, UPLIFTING MUSIC, BOOK)
- ☐ 16oz GLASS OF WATER
- ☐ STRETCH MY BODY
- ☐ GREEN SMOOTHIE
- ☐ PRAY OR MEDITATE 2-5 MINS
- ☐ MORNING SUPPLEMENTS OR ESSENTIAL OILS
- ☐ DRESSED AND STYLED FOR SUCCESS, FULL BODY SKIN CARE DONE

I CAN VISUALIZE MY BODY AND HEALTH…

I CAN VISUALIZE MY RELATIONSHIPS…

3 WORDS I WANT PEOPLE TO DESCRIBE ME AS…

NOTES AND IDEAS

_____

_____

_____

_____

5 THINGS I'M GRATEFUL FOR THIS MORNING

_____

_____

_____

_____

5 BIGGEST ACHIEVEMENTS OF MY LIFE

_____

_____

_____

_____

5 TARGETS FOR TODAY

THE GOAL I'M WORKING ON FIRST:

_____

TODAY'S PROMISE TO MYSELF:

_____

TODAY'S MOVEMENT OR WORKOUT GOAL:

_____

TODAY'S AFFIRMATION:

_____

ONE ACTION I'LL TAKE TODAY TO MOVE TOWARDS MY FIRST GOAL:

_____

MORNING CHECKLIST

- ☐ DO NOT TOUCH CELL PHONE FOR MINIMUM 20 MINS
- ☐ TEA OR COFFEE
- ☐ 5 MINS POSITIVE CONTENT (PODCAST, UPLIFTING MUSIC, BOOK)
- ☐ 16oz GLASS OF WATER
- ☐ STRETCH MY BODY
- ☐ GREEN SMOOTHIE
- ☐ PRAY OR MEDITATE 2-5 MINS
- ☐ MORNING SUPPLEMENTS OR ESSENTIAL OILS
- ☐ DRESSED AND STYLED FOR SUCCESS, FULL BODY SKIN CARE DONE

I CAN VISUALIZE MY BODY AND HEALTH...

I CAN VISUALIZE MY RELATIONSHIPS...

3 WORDS I WANT PEOPLE TO DESCRIBE ME AS...

NOTES AND IDEAS

_____

_____

_____

_____

5 | THINGS I'M GRATEFUL FOR THIS MORNING

_____

_____

_____

_____

_____

5 | BIGGEST ACHIEVEMENTS OF MY LIFE

_____

_____

_____

_____

_____

5 | TARGETS FOR TODAY

THE GOAL I'M WORKING ON FIRST:

_____

TODAY'S PROMISE TO MYSELF:

_____

TODAY'S MOVEMENT OR WORKOUT GOAL:

_____

TODAY'S AFFIRMATION:

_____

ONE ACTION I'LL TAKE TODAY TO MOVE TOWARDS MY FIRST GOAL:

_____

MORNING CHECKLIST

- [ ] DO NOT TOUCH CELL PHONE FOR MINIMUM 20 MINS
- [ ] TEA OR COFFEE
- [ ] 5 MINS POSITIVE CONTENT (PODCAST, UPLIFTING MUSIC, BOOK)
- [ ] 16oz GLASS OF WATER
- [ ] STRETCH MY BODY
- [ ] GREEN SMOOTHIE
- [ ] PRAY OR MEDITATE 2-5 MINS
- [ ] MORNING SUPPLEMENTS OR ESSENTIAL OILS
- [ ] DRESSED AND STYLED FOR SUCCESS, FULL BODY SKIN CARE DONE

I CAN VISUALIZE MY BODY AND HEALTH...

I CAN VISUALIZE MY RELATIONSHIPS...

3 WORDS I WANT PEOPLE TO DESCRIBE ME AS...

NOTES AND IDEAS

_____

_____

_____

_____

5 THINGS I'M GRATEFUL FOR THIS MORNING

_____

_____

_____

_____

5 BIGGEST ACHIEVEMENTS OF MY LIFE

_____

_____

_____

_____

5 TARGETS FOR TODAY

THE GOAL I'M WORKING ON FIRST:

_____

TODAY'S PROMISE TO MYSELF:

_____

TODAY'S MOVEMENT OR WORKOUT GOAL:

_____

TODAY'S AFFIRMATION:

_____

ONE ACTION I'LL TAKE TODAY TO MOVE TOWARDS MY FIRST GOAL:

_____

MORNING CHECKLIST

- ☐ DO NOT TOUCH CELL PHONE FOR MINIMUM 20 MINS
- ☐ TEA OR COFFEE
- ☐ 5 MINS POSITIVE CONTENT (PODCAST, UPLIFTING MUSIC, BOOK)
- ☐ 16oz GLASS OF WATER
- ☐ STRETCH MY BODY
- ☐ GREEN SMOOTHIE
- ☐ PRAY OR MEDITATE 2-5 MINS
- ☐ MORNING SUPPLEMENTS OR ESSENTIAL OILS
- ☐ DRESSED AND STYLED FOR SUCCESS, FULL BODY SKIN CARE DONE

I CAN VISUALIZE MY BODY AND HEALTH...

I CAN VISUALIZE MY RELATIONSHIPS...

3 WORDS I WANT PEOPLE TO DESCRIBE ME AS...

NOTES AND IDEAS

_____

_____

_____

_____

5 THINGS I'M GRATEFUL FOR THIS MORNING

_____

_____

_____

_____

_____

5 BIGGEST ACHIEVEMENTS OF MY LIFE

_____

_____

_____

_____

_____

5 TARGETS FOR TODAY

THE GOAL I'M WORKING ON FIRST:

_____

TODAY'S PROMISE TO MYSELF:

_____

TODAY'S MOVEMENT OR WORKOUT GOAL:

_____

TODAY'S AFFIRMATION:

_____

ONE ACTION I'LL TAKE TODAY TO MOVE TOWARDS MY FIRST GOAL:

_____

MORNING CHECKLIST

- ☐ DO NOT TOUCH CELL PHONE FOR MINIMUM 20 MINS
- ☐ TEA OR COFFEE
- ☐ 5 MINS POSITIVE CONTENT (PODCAST, UPLIFTING MUSIC, BOOK)
- ☐ 16oz GLASS OF WATER
- ☐ STRETCH MY BODY
- ☐ GREEN SMOOTHIE
- ☐ PRAY OR MEDITATE 2-5 MINS
- ☐ MORNING SUPPLEMENTS OR ESSENTIAL OILS
- ☐ DRESSED AND STYLED FOR SUCCESS, FULL BODY SKIN CARE DONE

I CAN VISUALIZE MY BODY AND HEALTH…

I CAN VISUALIZE MY RELATIONSHIPS…

3 WORDS I WANT PEOPLE TO DESCRIBE ME AS…

NOTES AND IDEAS

_____

_____

_____

_____

5 THINGS I'M GRATEFUL FOR
THIS MORNING

5 BIGGEST ACHIEVEMENTS
OF MY LIFE

_____

_____

_____

_____

_____

_____

_____

_____

_____

_____

5 TARGETS FOR TODAY

THE GOAL I'M WORKING ON FIRST:

_____

TODAY'S PROMISE TO MYSELF:

_____

TODAY'S MOVEMENT OR WORKOUT GOAL:

_____

TODAY'S AFFIRMATION:

_____

ONE ACTION I'LL TAKE TODAY TO MOVE TOWARDS MY FIRST GOAL:

_____

MORNING CHECKLIST

- ☐ DO NOT TOUCH CELL PHONE FOR MINIMUM 20 MINS
- ☐ TEA OR COFFEE
- ☐ 5 MINS POSITIVE CONTENT (PODCAST, UPLIFTING MUSIC, BOOK)
- ☐ 16oz GLASS OF WATER
- ☐ STRETCH MY BODY
- ☐ GREEN SMOOTHIE
- ☐ PRAY OR MEDITATE 2-5 MINS
- ☐ MORNING SUPPLEMENTS OR ESSENTIAL OILS
- ☐ DRESSED AND STYLED FOR SUCCESS, FULL BODY SKIN CARE DONE

I CAN VISUALIZE MY BODY AND HEALTH...

I CAN VISUALIZE MY RELATIONSHIPS...

3 WORDS I WANT PEOPLE TO DESCRIBE ME AS...

NOTES AND IDEAS

_____

_____

_____

_____

5 THINGS I'M GRATEFUL FOR THIS MORNING

_____

_____

_____

_____

_____

5 BIGGEST ACHIEVEMENTS OF MY LIFE

_____

_____

_____

_____

5 TARGETS FOR TODAY

THE GOAL I'M WORKING ON FIRST:

_____

TODAY'S PROMISE TO MYSELF:

_____

TODAY'S MOVEMENT OR WORKOUT GOAL:

_____

TODAY'S AFFIRMATION:

_____

ONE ACTION I'LL TAKE TODAY TO MOVE TOWARDS MY FIRST GOAL:

_____

MORNING CHECKLIST

- ☐ DO NOT TOUCH CELL PHONE FOR MINIMUM 20 MINS
- ☐ TEA OR COFFEE
- ☐ 5 MINS POSITIVE CONTENT (PODCAST, UPLIFTING MUSIC, BOOK)
- ☐ 16oz GLASS OF WATER
- ☐ STRETCH MY BODY
- ☐ GREEN SMOOTHIE
- ☐ PRAY OR MEDITATE 2-5 MINS
- ☐ MORNING SUPPLEMENTS OR ESSENTIAL OILS
- ☐ DRESSED AND STYLED FOR SUCCESS, FULL BODY SKIN CARE DONE

I CAN VISUALIZE MY BODY AND HEALTH…

I CAN VISUALIZE MY RELATIONSHIPS…

3 WORDS I WANT PEOPLE TO DESCRIBE ME AS…

NOTES AND IDEAS

_____

_____

_____

_____

5 | THINGS I'M GRATEFUL FOR THIS MORNING

---

5 | BIGGEST ACHIEVEMENTS OF MY LIFE

---

5 | TARGETS FOR TODAY

THE GOAL I'M WORKING ON FIRST:

_____

TODAY'S PROMISE TO MYSELF:

_____

TODAY'S MOVEMENT OR WORKOUT GOAL:

_____

TODAY'S AFFIRMATION:

_____

ONE ACTION I'LL TAKE TODAY TO MOVE TOWARDS MY FIRST GOAL:

_____

MORNING CHECKLIST

- [ ] DO NOT TOUCH CELL PHONE FOR MINIMUM 20 MINS
- [ ] TEA OR COFFEE
- [ ] 5 MINS POSITIVE CONTENT (PODCAST, UPLIFTING MUSIC, BOOK)
- [ ] 16oz GLASS OF WATER
- [ ] STRETCH MY BODY
- [ ] GREEN SMOOTHIE
- [ ] PRAY OR MEDITATE 2-5 MINS
- [ ] MORNING SUPPLEMENTS OR ESSENTIAL OILS
- [ ] DRESSED AND STYLED FOR SUCCESS, FULL BODY SKIN CARE DONE

I CAN VISUALIZE MY BODY AND HEALTH...

I CAN VISUALIZE MY RELATIONSHIPS...

3 WORDS I WANT PEOPLE TO DESCRIBE ME AS...

NOTES AND IDEAS

_____

_____

_____

_____

5 THINGS I'M GRATEFUL FOR THIS MORNING

_____

_____

_____

_____

_____

5 BIGGEST ACHIEVEMENTS OF MY LIFE

_____

_____

_____

_____

_____

5 TARGETS FOR TODAY

THE GOAL I'M WORKING ON FIRST:

_____

TODAY'S PROMISE TO MYSELF:

_____

TODAY'S MOVEMENT OR WORKOUT GOAL:

_____

TODAY'S AFFIRMATION:

_____

ONE ACTION I'LL TAKE TODAY TO MOVE TOWARDS MY FIRST GOAL:

_____

MORNING CHECKLIST

- ☐ DO NOT TOUCH CELL PHONE FOR MINIMUM 20 MINS
- ☐ TEA OR COFFEE
- ☐ 5 MINS POSITIVE CONTENT (PODCAST, UPLIFTING MUSIC, BOOK)
- ☐ 16oz GLASS OF WATER
- ☐ STRETCH MY BODY
- ☐ GREEN SMOOTHIE
- ☐ PRAY OR MEDITATE 2-5 MINS
- ☐ MORNING SUPPLEMENTS OR ESSENTIAL OILS
- ☐ DRESSED AND STYLED FOR SUCCESS, FULL BODY SKIN CARE DONE

I CAN VISUALIZE MY BODY AND HEALTH...

I CAN VISUALIZE MY RELATIONSHIPS...

3 WORDS I WANT PEOPLE TO DESCRIBE ME AS...

NOTES AND IDEAS

_____

_____

_____

_____

5 THINGS I'M GRATEFUL FOR THIS MORNING

_____

_____

_____

_____

5 BIGGEST ACHIEVEMENTS OF MY LIFE

_____

_____

_____

_____

5 TARGETS FOR TODAY

THE GOAL I'M WORKING ON FIRST:

_____

TODAY'S PROMISE TO MYSELF:

_____

TODAY'S MOVEMENT OR WORKOUT GOAL:

_____

TODAY'S AFFIRMATION:

_____

ONE ACTION I'LL TAKE TODAY TO MOVE TOWARDS MY FIRST GOAL:

_____

MORNING CHECKLIST

- ☐ DO NOT TOUCH CELL PHONE FOR MINIMUM 20 MINS
- ☐ TEA OR COFFEE
- ☐ 5 MINS POSITIVE CONTENT (PODCAST, UPLIFTING MUSIC, BOOK)
- ☐ 16oz GLASS OF WATER
- ☐ STRETCH MY BODY
- ☐ GREEN SMOOTHIE
- ☐ PRAY OR MEDITATE 2-5 MINS
- ☐ MORNING SUPPLEMENTS OR ESSENTIAL OILS
- ☐ DRESSED AND STYLED FOR SUCCESS, FULL BODY SKIN CARE DONE

I CAN VISUALIZE MY BODY AND HEALTH...

I CAN VISUALIZE MY RELATIONSHIPS...

3 WORDS I WANT PEOPLE TO DESCRIBE ME AS...

NOTES AND IDEAS

_____

_____

_____

_____

5 THINGS I'M GRATEFUL FOR THIS MORNING

_____

_____

_____

_____

_____

5 BIGGEST ACHIEVEMENTS OF MY LIFE

_____

_____

_____

_____

_____

5 TARGETS FOR TODAY

THE GOAL I'M WORKING ON FIRST:

_____

TODAY'S PROMISE TO MYSELF:

_____

TODAY'S MOVEMENT OR WORKOUT GOAL:

_____

TODAY'S AFFIRMATION:

_____

ONE ACTION I'LL TAKE TODAY TO MOVE TOWARDS MY FIRST GOAL:

_____

MORNING CHECKLIST

- ☐ DO NOT TOUCH CELL PHONE FOR MINIMUM 20 MINS
- ☐ TEA OR COFFEE
- ☐ 5 MINS POSITIVE CONTENT (PODCAST, UPLIFTING MUSIC, BOOK)
- ☐ 16oz GLASS OF WATER
- ☐ STRETCH MY BODY
- ☐ GREEN SMOOTHIE
- ☐ PRAY OR MEDITATE 2-5 MINS
- ☐ MORNING SUPPLEMENTS OR ESSENTIAL OILS
- ☐ DRESSED AND STYLED FOR SUCCESS, FULL BODY SKIN CARE DONE

I CAN VISUALIZE MY BODY AND HEALTH...

I CAN VISUALIZE MY RELATIONSHIPS...

3 WORDS I WANT PEOPLE TO DESCRIBE ME AS...

NOTES AND IDEAS

_____

_____

_____

_____

5 | THINGS I'M GRATEFUL FOR THIS MORNING

_____

_____

_____

_____

_____

5 | BIGGEST ACHIEVEMENTS OF MY LIFE

_____

_____

_____

_____

_____

5 | TARGETS FOR TODAY

THE GOAL I'M WORKING ON FIRST:

_____

TODAY'S PROMISE TO MYSELF:

_____

TODAY'S MOVEMENT OR WORKOUT GOAL:

_____

TODAY'S AFFIRMATION:

_____

ONE ACTION I'LL TAKE TODAY TO MOVE TOWARDS MY FIRST GOAL:

_____

MORNING CHECKLIST

- ☐ DO NOT TOUCH CELL PHONE FOR MINIMUM 20 MINS
- ☐ TEA OR COFFEE
- ☐ 5 MINS POSITIVE CONTENT (PODCAST, UPLIFTING MUSIC, BOOK)
- ☐ 16oz GLASS OF WATER
- ☐ STRETCH MY BODY
- ☐ GREEN SMOOTHIE
- ☐ PRAY OR MEDITATE 2-5 MINS
- ☐ MORNING SUPPLEMENTS OR ESSENTIAL OILS
- ☐ DRESSED AND STYLED FOR SUCCESS, FULL BODY SKIN CARE DONE

I CAN VISUALIZE MY BODY AND HEALTH…

I CAN VISUALIZE MY RELATIONSHIPS…

3 WORDS I WANT PEOPLE TO DESCRIBE ME AS…

NOTES AND IDEAS

_____

_____

_____

_____

5 THINGS I'M GRATEFUL FOR THIS MORNING

_____

_____

_____

_____

5 BIGGEST ACHIEVEMENTS OF MY LIFE

_____

_____

_____

_____

5 TARGETS FOR TODAY

THE GOAL I'M WORKING ON FIRST:

_____

TODAY'S PROMISE TO MYSELF:

_____

TODAY'S MOVEMENT OR WORKOUT GOAL:

_____

TODAY'S AFFIRMATION:

_____

ONE ACTION I'LL TAKE TODAY TO MOVE TOWARDS MY FIRST GOAL:

_____

MORNING CHECKLIST

- ☐ DO NOT TOUCH CELL PHONE FOR MINIMUM 20 MINS
- ☐ TEA OR COFFEE
- ☐ 5 MINS POSITIVE CONTENT (PODCAST, UPLIFTING MUSIC, BOOK)
- ☐ 16oz GLASS OF WATER
- ☐ STRETCH MY BODY
- ☐ GREEN SMOOTHIE
- ☐ PRAY OR MEDITATE 2-5 MINS
- ☐ MORNING SUPPLEMENTS OR ESSENTIAL OILS
- ☐ DRESSED AND STYLED FOR SUCCESS, FULL BODY SKIN CARE DONE

I CAN VISUALIZE MY BODY AND HEALTH...

I CAN VISUALIZE MY RELATIONSHIPS...

3 WORDS I WANT PEOPLE TO DESCRIBE ME AS...

NOTES AND IDEAS

_____

_____

_____

_____

5 | THINGS I'M GRATEFUL FOR THIS MORNING

_____

_____

_____

_____

_____

5 | BIGGEST ACHIEVEMENTS OF MY LIFE

_____

_____

_____

_____

5 | TARGETS FOR TODAY

THE GOAL I'M WORKING ON FIRST:

_____

TODAY'S PROMISE TO MYSELF:

_____

TODAY'S MOVEMENT OR WORKOUT GOAL:

_____

TODAY'S AFFIRMATION:

_____

ONE ACTION I'LL TAKE TODAY TO MOVE TOWARDS MY FIRST GOAL:

_____

MORNING CHECKLIST

- ☐ DO NOT TOUCH CELL PHONE FOR MINIMUM 20 MINS
- ☐ TEA OR COFFEE
- ☐ 5 MINS POSITIVE CONTENT (PODCAST, UPLIFTING MUSIC, BOOK)
- ☐ 16oz GLASS OF WATER
- ☐ STRETCH MY BODY
- ☐ GREEN SMOOTHIE
- ☐ PRAY OR MEDITATE 2-5 MINS
- ☐ MORNING SUPPLEMENTS OR ESSENTIAL OILS
- ☐ DRESSED AND STYLED FOR SUCCESS, FULL BODY SKIN CARE DONE

I CAN VISUALIZE MY BODY AND HEALTH…

I CAN VISUALIZE MY RELATIONSHIPS…

3 WORDS I WANT PEOPLE TO DESCRIBE ME AS…

NOTES AND IDEAS

_____

_____

_____

_____

5 THINGS I'M GRATEFUL FOR THIS MORNING

_____

_____

_____

_____

_____

5 BIGGEST ACHIEVEMENTS OF MY LIFE

_____

_____

_____

_____

_____

5 TARGETS FOR TODAY

THE GOAL I'M WORKING ON FIRST:

_____

TODAY'S PROMISE TO MYSELF:

_____

TODAY'S MOVEMENT OR WORKOUT GOAL:

_____

TODAY'S AFFIRMATION:

_____

ONE ACTION I'LL TAKE TODAY TO MOVE TOWARDS MY FIRST GOAL:

_____

MORNING CHECKLIST

- ☐ DO NOT TOUCH CELL PHONE FOR MINIMUM 20 MINS
- ☐ TEA OR COFFEE
- ☐ 5 MINS POSITIVE CONTENT (PODCAST, UPLIFTING MUSIC, BOOK)
- ☐ 16oz GLASS OF WATER
- ☐ STRETCH MY BODY
- ☐ GREEN SMOOTHIE
- ☐ PRAY OR MEDITATE 2-5 MINS
- ☐ MORNING SUPPLEMENTS OR ESSENTIAL OILS
- ☐ DRESSED AND STYLED FOR SUCCESS, FULL BODY SKIN CARE DONE

I CAN VISUALIZE MY BODY AND HEALTH…

I CAN VISUALIZE MY RELATIONSHIPS…

3 WORDS I WANT PEOPLE TO DESCRIBE ME AS…

NOTES AND IDEAS

_____

_____

_____

_____

5 THINGS I'M GRATEFUL FOR THIS MORNING

_____

_____

_____

_____

_____

5 BIGGEST ACHIEVEMENTS OF MY LIFE

_____

_____

_____

_____

_____

5 TARGETS FOR TODAY

THE GOAL I'M WORKING ON FIRST:

_____

TODAY'S PROMISE TO MYSELF:

_____

TODAY'S MOVEMENT OR WORKOUT GOAL:

_____

TODAY'S AFFIRMATION:

_____

ONE ACTION I'LL TAKE TODAY TO MOVE TOWARDS MY FIRST GOAL:

_____

MORNING CHECKLIST

- ☐ DO NOT TOUCH CELL PHONE FOR MINIMUM 20 MINS
- ☐ TEA OR COFFEE
- ☐ 5 MINS POSITIVE CONTENT (PODCAST, UPLIFTING MUSIC, BOOK)
- ☐ 16oz GLASS OF WATER
- ☐ STRETCH MY BODY
- ☐ GREEN SMOOTHIE
- ☐ PRAY OR MEDITATE 2-5 MINS
- ☐ MORNING SUPPLEMENTS OR ESSENTIAL OILS
- ☐ DRESSED AND STYLED FOR SUCCESS, FULL BODY SKIN CARE DONE

I CAN VISUALIZE MY BODY AND HEALTH...

I CAN VISUALIZE MY RELATIONSHIPS...

3 WORDS I WANT PEOPLE TO DESCRIBE ME AS...

NOTES AND IDEAS

_____

_____

_____

_____

5 THINGS I'M GRATEFUL FOR THIS MORNING

---

5 BIGGEST ACHIEVEMENTS OF MY LIFE

---

5 TARGETS FOR TODAY

THE GOAL I'M WORKING ON FIRST:

_____

TODAY'S PROMISE TO MYSELF:

_____

TODAY'S MOVEMENT OR WORKOUT GOAL:

_____

TODAY'S AFFIRMATION:

_____

ONE ACTION I'LL TAKE TODAY TO MOVE TOWARDS MY FIRST GOAL:

_____

MORNING CHECKLIST

- ☐ DO NOT TOUCH CELL PHONE FOR MINIMUM 20 MINS
- ☐ TEA OR COFFEE
- ☐ 5 MINS POSITIVE CONTENT (PODCAST, UPLIFTING MUSIC, BOOK)
- ☐ 16oz GLASS OF WATER
- ☐ STRETCH MY BODY
- ☐ GREEN SMOOTHIE
- ☐ PRAY OR MEDITATE 2-5 MINS
- ☐ MORNING SUPPLEMENTS OR ESSENTIAL OILS
- ☐ DRESSED AND STYLED FOR SUCCESS, FULL BODY SKIN CARE DONE

I CAN VISUALIZE MY BODY AND HEALTH…

I CAN VISUALIZE MY RELATIONSHIPS…

3 WORDS I WANT PEOPLE TO DESCRIBE ME AS…

NOTES AND IDEAS

_____

_____

_____

_____

5 | THINGS I'M GRATEFUL FOR THIS MORNING

_____

_____

_____

_____

_____

5 | BIGGEST ACHIEVEMENTS OF MY LIFE

_____

_____

_____

_____

_____

5 | TARGETS FOR TODAY

THE GOAL I'M WORKING ON FIRST:

_____

TODAY'S PROMISE TO MYSELF:

_____

TODAY'S MOVEMENT OR WORKOUT GOAL:

_____

TODAY'S AFFIRMATION:

_____

ONE ACTION I'LL TAKE TODAY TO MOVE TOWARDS MY FIRST GOAL:

_____

MORNING CHECKLIST

- ☐ DO NOT TOUCH CELL PHONE FOR MINIMUM 20 MINS
- ☐ TEA OR COFFEE
- ☐ 5 MINS POSITIVE CONTENT (PODCAST, UPLIFTING MUSIC, BOOK)
- ☐ 16oz GLASS OF WATER
- ☐ STRETCH MY BODY
- ☐ GREEN SMOOTHIE
- ☐ PRAY OR MEDITATE 2-5 MINS
- ☐ MORNING SUPPLEMENTS OR ESSENTIAL OILS
- ☐ DRESSED AND STYLED FOR SUCCESS, FULL BODY SKIN CARE DONE

I CAN VISUALIZE MY BODY AND HEALTH…

I CAN VISUALIZE MY RELATIONSHIPS…

3 WORDS I WANT PEOPLE TO DESCRIBE ME AS…

NOTES AND IDEAS

_____

_____

_____

_____

5 | THINGS I'M GRATEFUL FOR THIS MORNING

_____

_____

_____

_____

_____

5 | BIGGEST ACHIEVEMENTS OF MY LIFE

_____

_____

_____

_____

_____

5 | TARGETS FOR TODAY

THE GOAL I'M WORKING ON FIRST:

_____

TODAY'S PROMISE TO MYSELF:

_____

TODAY'S MOVEMENT OR WORKOUT GOAL:

_____

TODAY'S AFFIRMATION:

_____

ONE ACTION I'LL TAKE TODAY TO MOVE TOWARDS MY FIRST GOAL:

_____

MORNING CHECKLIST

- ☐ DO NOT TOUCH CELL PHONE FOR MINIMUM 20 MINS
- ☐ TEA OR COFFEE
- ☐ 5 MINS POSITIVE CONTENT (PODCAST, UPLIFTING MUSIC, BOOK)
- ☐ 16oz GLASS OF WATER
- ☐ STRETCH MY BODY
- ☐ GREEN SMOOTHIE
- ☐ PRAY OR MEDITATE 2-5 MINS
- ☐ MORNING SUPPLEMENTS OR ESSENTIAL OILS
- ☐ DRESSED AND STYLED FOR SUCCESS, FULL BODY SKIN CARE DONE

I CAN VISUALIZE MY BODY AND HEALTH…

I CAN VISUALIZE MY RELATIONSHIPS…

3 WORDS I WANT PEOPLE TO DESCRIBE ME AS…

NOTES AND IDEAS

_____

_____

_____

_____

5 THINGS I'M GRATEFUL FOR THIS MORNING

_____

_____

_____

_____

_____

5 BIGGEST ACHIEVEMENTS OF MY LIFE

_____

_____

_____

_____

_____

5 TARGETS FOR TODAY

THE GOAL I'M WORKING ON FIRST:

_____

TODAY'S PROMISE TO MYSELF:

_____

TODAY'S MOVEMENT OR WORKOUT GOAL:

_____

TODAY'S AFFIRMATION:

_____

ONE ACTION I'LL TAKE TODAY TO MOVE TOWARDS MY FIRST GOAL:

_____

MORNING CHECKLIST

- [ ] DO NOT TOUCH CELL PHONE FOR MINIMUM 20 MINS
- [ ] TEA OR COFFEE
- [ ] 5 MINS POSITIVE CONTENT (PODCAST, UPLIFTING MUSIC, BOOK)
- [ ] 16oz GLASS OF WATER
- [ ] STRETCH MY BODY
- [ ] GREEN SMOOTHIE
- [ ] PRAY OR MEDITATE 2-5 MINS
- [ ] MORNING SUPPLEMENTS OR ESSENTIAL OILS
- [ ] DRESSED AND STYLED FOR SUCCESS, FULL BODY SKIN CARE DONE

I CAN VISUALIZE MY BODY AND HEALTH...

I CAN VISUALIZE MY RELATIONSHIPS...

3 WORDS I WANT PEOPLE TO DESCRIBE ME AS...

NOTES AND IDEAS

_____

_____

_____

_____

5 | THINGS I'M GRATEFUL FOR THIS MORNING

_____

_____

_____

_____

_____

5 | BIGGEST ACHIEVEMENTS OF MY LIFE

_____

_____

_____

_____

_____

5 | TARGETS FOR TODAY

THE GOAL I'M WORKING ON FIRST:

_____

TODAY'S PROMISE TO MYSELF:

_____

TODAY'S MOVEMENT OR WORKOUT GOAL:

_____

TODAY'S AFFIRMATION:

_____

ONE ACTION I'LL TAKE TODAY TO MOVE TOWARDS MY FIRST GOAL:

_____

MORNING CHECKLIST

- [ ] DO NOT TOUCH CELL PHONE FOR MINIMUM 20 MINS
- [ ] TEA OR COFFEE
- [ ] 5 MINS POSITIVE CONTENT (PODCAST, UPLIFTING MUSIC, BOOK)
- [ ] 16oz GLASS OF WATER
- [ ] STRETCH MY BODY
- [ ] GREEN SMOOTHIE
- [ ] PRAY OR MEDITATE 2-5 MINS
- [ ] MORNING SUPPLEMENTS OR ESSENTIAL OILS
- [ ] DRESSED AND STYLED FOR SUCCESS, FULL BODY SKIN CARE DONE

I CAN VISUALIZE MY BODY AND HEALTH…

I CAN VISUALIZE MY RELATIONSHIPS…

3 WORDS I WANT PEOPLE TO DESCRIBE ME AS…

NOTES AND IDEAS

_____

_____

_____

_____

5 | THINGS I'M GRATEFUL FOR THIS MORNING

---

5 | BIGGEST ACHIEVEMENTS OF MY LIFE

---

5 | TARGETS FOR TODAY

THE GOAL I'M WORKING ON FIRST:

TODAY'S PROMISE TO MYSELF:

TODAY'S MOVEMENT OR WORKOUT GOAL:

TODAY'S AFFIRMATION:

ONE ACTION I'LL TAKE TODAY TO MOVE TOWARDS MY FIRST GOAL:

MORNING CHECKLIST

- [ ] DO NOT TOUCH CELL PHONE FOR MINIMUM 20 MINS
- [ ] TEA OR COFFEE
- [ ] 5 MINS POSITIVE CONTENT (PODCAST, UPLIFTING MUSIC, BOOK)
- [ ] 16oz GLASS OF WATER
- [ ] STRETCH MY BODY
- [ ] GREEN SMOOTHIE
- [ ] PRAY OR MEDITATE 2-5 MINS
- [ ] MORNING SUPPLEMENTS OR ESSENTIAL OILS
- [ ] DRESSED AND STYLED FOR SUCCESS, FULL BODY SKIN CARE DONE

I CAN VISUALIZE MY BODY AND HEALTH…

I CAN VISUALIZE MY RELATIONSHIPS…

3 WORDS I WANT PEOPLE TO DESCRIBE ME AS…

NOTES AND IDEAS

_____

_____

_____

_____

5 THINGS I'M GRATEFUL FOR THIS MORNING

5 BIGGEST ACHIEVEMENTS OF MY LIFE

_____

_____

_____

_____

_____

_____

_____

_____

_____

_____

5 TARGETS FOR TODAY

THE GOAL I'M WORKING ON FIRST:

_____

TODAY'S PROMISE TO MYSELF:

_____

TODAY'S MOVEMENT OR WORKOUT GOAL:

_____

TODAY'S AFFIRMATION:

_____

ONE ACTION I'LL TAKE TODAY TO MOVE TOWARDS MY FIRST GOAL:

_____

MORNING CHECKLIST

- ☐ DO NOT TOUCH CELL PHONE FOR MINIMUM 20 MINS
- ☐ TEA OR COFFEE
- ☐ 5 MINS POSITIVE CONTENT (PODCAST, UPLIFTING MUSIC, BOOK)
- ☐ 16oz GLASS OF WATER
- ☐ STRETCH MY BODY
- ☐ GREEN SMOOTHIE
- ☐ PRAY OR MEDITATE 2-5 MINS
- ☐ MORNING SUPPLEMENTS OR ESSENTIAL OILS
- ☐ DRESSED AND STYLED FOR SUCCESS, FULL BODY SKIN CARE DONE

I CAN VISUALIZE MY BODY AND HEALTH...

I CAN VISUALIZE MY RELATIONSHIPS...

3 WORDS I WANT PEOPLE TO DESCRIBE ME AS...

NOTES AND IDEAS

_____

_____

_____

_____

5 | THINGS I'M GRATEFUL FOR THIS MORNING

_____

_____

_____

_____

5 | BIGGEST ACHIEVEMENTS OF MY LIFE

_____

_____

_____

_____

5 | TARGETS FOR TODAY

THE GOAL I'M WORKING ON FIRST:

_____

TODAY'S PROMISE TO MYSELF:

_____

TODAY'S MOVEMENT OR WORKOUT GOAL:

_____

TODAY'S AFFIRMATION:

_____

ONE ACTION I'LL TAKE TODAY TO MOVE TOWARDS MY FIRST GOAL:

_____

MORNING CHECKLIST

- [ ] DO NOT TOUCH CELL PHONE FOR MINIMUM 20 MINS
- [ ] TEA OR COFFEE
- [ ] 5 MINS POSITIVE CONTENT (PODCAST, UPLIFTING MUSIC, BOOK)
- [ ] 16oz GLASS OF WATER
- [ ] STRETCH MY BODY
- [ ] GREEN SMOOTHIE
- [ ] PRAY OR MEDITATE 2-5 MINS
- [ ] MORNING SUPPLEMENTS OR ESSENTIAL OILS
- [ ] DRESSED AND STYLED FOR SUCCESS, FULL BODY SKIN CARE DONE

I CAN VISUALIZE MY BODY AND HEALTH…

I CAN VISUALIZE MY RELATIONSHIPS…

3 WORDS I WANT PEOPLE TO DESCRIBE ME AS…

NOTES AND IDEAS

_____

_____

_____

_____

5 | THINGS I'M GRATEFUL FOR THIS MORNING

_____

_____

_____

_____

_____

5 | BIGGEST ACHIEVEMENTS OF MY LIFE

_____

_____

_____

_____

_____

5 | TARGETS FOR TODAY

THE GOAL I'M WORKING ON FIRST:

_____

TODAY'S PROMISE TO MYSELF:

_____

TODAY'S MOVEMENT OR WORKOUT GOAL:

_____

TODAY'S AFFIRMATION:

_____

ONE ACTION I'LL TAKE TODAY TO MOVE TOWARDS MY FIRST GOAL:

_____

MORNING CHECKLIST

- ☐ DO NOT TOUCH CELL PHONE FOR MINIMUM 20 MINS
- ☐ TEA OR COFFEE
- ☐ 5 MINS POSITIVE CONTENT (PODCAST, UPLIFTING MUSIC, BOOK)
- ☐ 16oz GLASS OF WATER
- ☐ STRETCH MY BODY
- ☐ GREEN SMOOTHIE
- ☐ PRAY OR MEDITATE 2-5 MINS
- ☐ MORNING SUPPLEMENTS OR ESSENTIAL OILS
- ☐ DRESSED AND STYLED FOR SUCCESS, FULL BODY SKIN CARE DONE

I CAN VISUALIZE MY BODY AND HEALTH...

I CAN VISUALIZE MY RELATIONSHIPS...

3 WORDS I WANT PEOPLE TO DESCRIBE ME AS...

NOTES AND IDEAS

_____

_____

_____

_____

5 | THINGS I'M GRATEFUL FOR THIS MORNING

_____

_____

_____

_____

_____

5 | BIGGEST ACHIEVEMENTS OF MY LIFE

_____

_____

_____

_____

_____

5 | TARGETS FOR TODAY

THE GOAL I'M WORKING ON FIRST:

_____

TODAY'S PROMISE TO MYSELF:

_____

TODAY'S MOVEMENT OR WORKOUT GOAL:

_____

TODAY'S AFFIRMATION:

_____

ONE ACTION I'LL TAKE TODAY TO MOVE TOWARDS MY FIRST GOAL:

_____

MORNING CHECKLIST

- ☐ DO NOT TOUCH CELL PHONE FOR MINIMUM 20 MINS
- ☐ TEA OR COFFEE
- ☐ 5 MINS POSITIVE CONTENT (PODCAST, UPLIFTING MUSIC, BOOK)
- ☐ 16oz GLASS OF WATER
- ☐ STRETCH MY BODY
- ☐ GREEN SMOOTHIE
- ☐ PRAY OR MEDITATE 2-5 MINS
- ☐ MORNING SUPPLEMENTS OR ESSENTIAL OILS
- ☐ DRESSED AND STYLED FOR SUCCESS, FULL BODY SKIN CARE DONE

I CAN VISUALIZE MY BODY AND HEALTH...

I CAN VISUALIZE MY RELATIONSHIPS...

3 WORDS I WANT PEOPLE TO DESCRIBE ME AS...

NOTES AND IDEAS

_____

_____

_____

_____

Made in the USA
San Bernardino, CA
21 April 2020